Acknowledgments

My thanks to my wife Brooke, to Joan Flynn for her help and support, to Peggy Larsen for design and Clark Marten for photography.

Front and back covers —

Details from *School Figures* by John Flynn.

Additional copies of this book may be ordered from:
Flynn Quilt Frame Company
1000 Shiloh Overpass Road
Billings, Montana 59106

ISBN 0-9627889-2-9

John Flynn's
Step-By-Step

Trapunto
&
Stippling

This book takes you through John Flynn's innovative new method for trapunto and his tips for successful stippling. Color photographs, patterns and design suggestions will help make your project a beautiful success.

CONTENTS

My "Star of Montana" quilt was my first try at stippling. This book is in large part a result of my search by trial and error for the secrets of stippled quilting. Here, I have my "Amish Wedding Ring" quilt on my Flynn Quilt Frame.
Star of Montana, 105" x 115"

2

Introduction

I attend every quilt show I can and appreciate all aspects of quilting. The quilts I invariably spent the most time admiring and, incidentally, the ones most often wearing blue ribbons are those with unique quilting designs or techniques—stippling, trapunto and fine feathers. These are the quilts that make me say, "I wish I had done that."

As a male quilter, I am asked a lot of questions about my quilting. The one question that needles me is that old favorite, "How long did it take you to do that?" I thoroughly enjoy quilting. The more quilting I can get on a quilt, the more I enjoy making that quilt and the more pleasure I ultimately get from it. This is a sustained pleasure. The satisfaction derived from an original artwork cannot be compared to the quick high of a short term project. I have fished all of my life and do not recall ever being asked how long it took to catch a particular trout. The pleasure is in the process and that pleasure is reflected in the final results.

In this book, I will take you step-by-step through the fine hand quilting techniques I have developed for pattern stippling and trapunto. I suggest that you read through the entire book before you begin your project. Pay special attention to the "Back to the Basics" section.

These techniques will not only enhance your quilting pleasure — they will stop quilt lovers in their tracks.

JFF Monogram, 24" x 30" oval, John Flynn.

 # rapunto

Traditionally, trapunto was done after a quilt was finished. The back of the quilt was slashed in the areas that needed stuffing, extra stuffing was added and then the slashes were hand-stitched closed. This seemed destructive and tedious to me and I started thinking about an alternative. I invented my Trapunto Rod, a tool which injects the extra stuffing in place between the layers during quilting. The rod is a clear plastic tube with a plunger. A bit of batting is loaded in the end, the rod is slipped between the quilt top and batting and directed to the area to be stuffed and injected. Step-by-step illustrations follow.

Before you begin quilting on a project, identify all areas that you want to enhance with trapunto. Areas to be stuffed can be divided into two categories — those like leaves, feathers, berries which will have batting added using the trapunto rod and narrow channels such as vines or stems which will be stuffed by cording.

Areas which are to be stuffed with the trapunto rod must be stuffed before you do any stippling. Areas to be corded are done last — after you have finished with the rod and finished any stippling — because it is difficult to quilt next to the corded ridge.

Ocean Waves, 30" x 30", John Flynn
Contrasting thread is effective here as outline,
but interferes with the stippling texture.

Christmas Wedding, detail, 18" double wedding ring, John Flynn.

Texas Star, 59" diameter, John Flynn.

Using the trapunto rod.

The first concern is stuffing the areas which will have
batting added with the trapunto rod. **It is critical that
you begin the process in the middle of your quilt
and work toward the edges** so that you don't
lock yourself out of an area.

First, quilt around the area
to be stuffed, leaving a 1/2" gap
that opens toward the side
of the frame.

Most feathers
can be quilted
in series and
stuffed all
at once

Cut a piece of standard weight
batting about the same size
as the area to be stuffed.
Even if you have chosen a
cotton batt, use poly batting
for the trapunto work because
it won't clump. It is a good idea
to test the poly batt — some brands
of poly will clump.

Insert the small piece of batting
into the end of the trapunto rod
— I use the point of my scissors.

With the batting in the rod,
slide the rod between the
top and the batting.

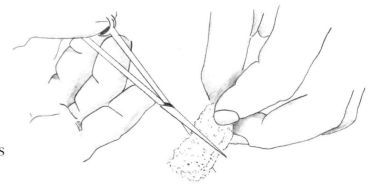

Guide it to the area to be stuffed. Note that the rod slips through your 3/4" basting stitches.

Push the end of the trapunto rod to inject the stuffing into the area you prepared. Pin the stuffing in the area you want it by sticking your needle through it and withdraw the trapunto rod.

Finish quilting around this area.

Work the stuffing around with your needle to smooth if necessary.

Once all of the trapunto is completed in an area, you can do the rest of the quilting, cording and stippling without worrying about quilting yourself out of an area that you need to get to with the rod.

Wyoming Star, 59" diameter, John Flynn
Machine quilting with trapunto.

Amish Wedding, detail, 9" double wedding ring, John Flynn

Cording

Materials. You will need a Tapestry Needle Size 24, a strong thread (quilting thread works well), and the yarn. I use 3 ply poly yarn and add or subtract plies as needed. The yarn will be double in the channel, so figure plies accordingly. Choose a yarn close to your batting in color so there isn't a color change which can be seen through your top fabric.

Remember, if you are planning to stipple, cording should be left until after the stippling is done.

Select the area to be corded. Don't try to do too long an area in one step — about 12" is tops. And, don't go too far along a curve — at most, do about half a circle at a time.

Cut a piece of thread about 3 times the length of the area to be corded.

Thread the tapestry needle with a double thread.

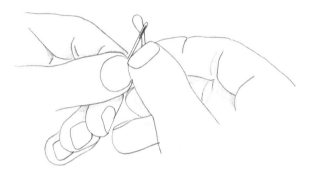

Beginning at one end of the channel to be corded, insert the needle its full length.

Pull the needle through leaving just the end of the needle's eye in the fabric.

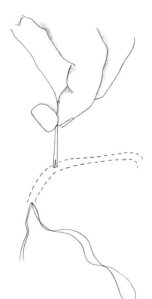

11

With the eye still in place, swing the needle
180° and continue to push it, eye end first,
through the channel.

Push the eye through fabric,
leaving just the tip in the fabric,
again swing the needle 180° and continue.
Repeat these steps until the end
of the channel is reached.

Pull the needle all the way through.
Hold onto the thread loop at the beginning
of the channel.

Cut a piece of yarn about 3 times
the length of the channel being stuffed.
Thread the yarn through the loop as
shown. The yarn will be double in the
channel so plan your number
of plies accordingly.

Pull both ends — the thread and the yarn —
to "sharpen" the end of the yarn in preparation
for pulling it through the channel.

Use the thread to pull the yarn
through the channel. Pull until
the yarn is almost to the end
of the channel, but do not pull
it through the fabric.

Cut excess yarn off at the
beginning end. Pull thread
at other end just enough
to bring the cut ends in.

Unthread the needle,
pull the thread out and discard.
Smooth the exit holes with your
fingernail or the tapestry needle.

Repeat until all channels
have been corded.

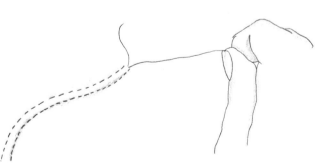

Star of Montana, detail (see page 2).

# *Stippling*

In engraving, to stipple is to engrave by means of dots or light strokes instead of lines, to use small short touches that produce an even and softly graded shadow. Stipple quilting can create the same interesting surface texture with variation in the size, placement and density of quilting stitches.

My first experience with stippling was not a complete success. I wanted to stipple the background around the feathered star on my "Star of Montana" quilt, page 2. I had no idea how to begin so I turned to Guild for advice. Some of the members had heard of it and one even had a second cousin whose friend knew someone whose sister had actually done it. Not much information there, so I went to my quilting books. From the one sentence I found, I learned that stippling is "a lot of quilting real close together." Armed with all of this information, I set out to stipple my first quilt. I decided to echo the star outline at 1/8" intervals to fill the lavender background pieces. By the time I finished the first triangular space, I realized that I was getting a lot of distortion. I didn't know why, but I knew I had distortion. After the second triangle, I realized that the longer quilting lines at the star edge of the triangle were pulling up the fabric more than the shorter lines near the outside of the area. (See detail, page 14.)

I had just learned my First Rule of Stippling…
DO NOT STIPPLE IN LONG PARALLEL LINES.

By the time I figured out what was happening, I had completed two of the triangles and decided to live with the distortion.

When I removed my quilt from the frame, all of my feather quilting melted into the stippling. I had learned another lesson the hard way!

The Second Rule of Stippling…
EVERY DESIGN ELEMENT YOU WANT TO REMAIN SMOOTH WITHIN THE STIPPLED AREA MUST BE STUFFED.

Even though this quilt remains one of my favorites, I knew it could have been better and I set out to learn more about stippling.

To test my new theories about stippling, I decided to make a sampler using different stippling patterns. My "School Figures" quilt (page 17) is the result of this study in stippling.

After outlining and stuffing all of the areas I wanted to remain smooth, I began to work on the stippling. To start, I intended to random stipple the entire background of the butterfly block. By the time I had done inside one wing, I realized that random was a very tedious process requiring incredible concentration. I finished the inside of the wings and switched to a checkerboard pattern for the rest of the block. I first drew a grid on the quilt. Then I filled each square with four rows of quilting, changing direction from horizontal to vertical in adjacent squares.

When the stippled texture began to appear, I discovered that it looked different where I had quilted adjacent lines of quilting "out of step" rather than "in step." I liked the wavy effect best and kept my stitches "out of step" on the remainder of the checkerboard.

STITCHES IN STEP

Now that I had figured out the benefits of using a grid, and learned to watch how my stitches were lining up, patterns developed quickly. Suddenly, stippling became relaxing and fun.

STITCHES OUT OF STEP

When you do stipple quilting, it is important to get the tension correct. The texture that develops when you stipple is the result of ridges between the stitches in adjacent rows of quilting. If the tension is not enough, the ridges will not develop and if the tension is too great, your quilt will gather and distort. The thread should be pulled just tight enough to set the stitches into the quilt. Most of the stippling patterns are done on grids which give you a reference to check for distortion.

TENSION

Stippling is not for everyone or for every quilt, but for that one time that it is necessary for the success of the project, you will need to know more than "it is a lot of quilting close together." I hope my suggestions will get you started and that soon you will be creating innovations of your own. Some of my favorite stippling patterns follow. Remember to be aware of how your stitches line up— "in step" or "out of step"—and use the resulting pattern to your best advantage.

School Figures, 36" x 54", John Flynn.
Natural "Kona," poly batt.

Note: Refer to the photo on page 17. Each motif is repeated 4 times in the individual block. The pattern for the frame used around each block is on page 39.

1/2"
GRID

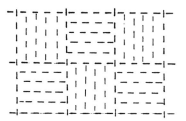

QUILT THE GRID LINES & FILL

CHECKERBOARD

The checkerboard is the simplest stippling pattern. Mark (or quilt using masking tape as a guide) a 1/2" grid on your quilt. Fill each square with four rows of quilting, changing direction from horizontal to vertical in adjacent squares.

There are many variations on this pattern — irregular grid, wavy grid, diamonds. Each will look different depending on whether your stitches are in- or out-of-step.

1/2" – 60°
GRID

QUILT THE GRID LINES & FILL

DIAMOND

Mark or quilt a 1/2" – 60° grid. Fill in each diamond with 4 lines
of quilting, changing directions in adjacent diamonds.

1/2"
GRID

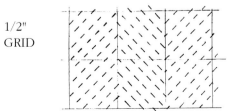

DO NOT QUILT THE GRID LINES

HERRINGBONE

The herringbone is the most popular of my stippling patterns. It is easy to recognize and it is one of the easier patterns to stipple because there is not much changing of stitch direction. The herringbone pattern is also stippled using a 1/2" grid as a guide. DO NOT QUILT THE GRID LINES FOR THIS PATTERN. Quilt a series of zigzag lines across the grid on a diagonal. The lines should be 1/8" apart on the vertical grid. In my original sampler, I used the 1/2" grid, but as with the checkerboard, the grid can be varied for many different looks.

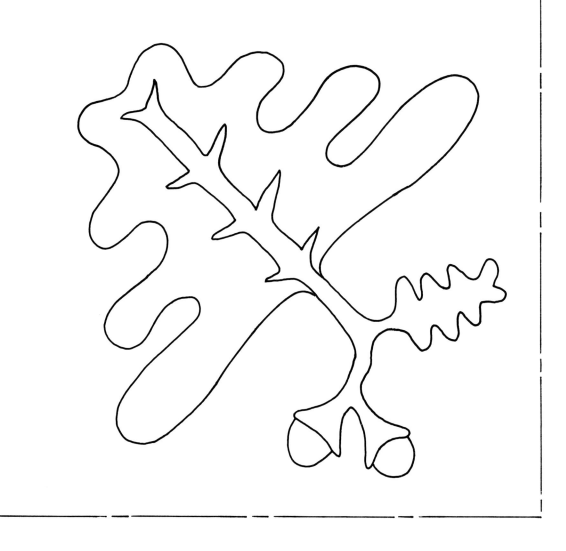

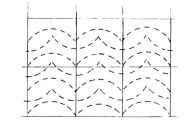

1/2"
GRID

24

"RANDOM"

This alternating scallops of this pattern produce a random look. Mark the 1/2" grid for a guide. DO NOT QUILT THE GRID. Quilt scallops arcing in one direction at 1/4" intervals on the vertical grid. Then quilt scallops arcing in the opposite direction to fill the space. This method of obtaining random-look quilting is easier for me than actual random. I have a pattern to follow and do not have to figure out where the next stitch is to go. When completed, the alternating scallop gives a pleasant stipple background without a discernible pattern — such as herringbone or checkerboard.

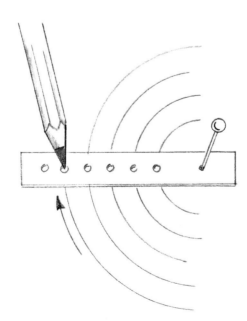

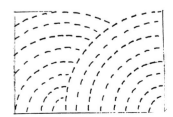

FAN

Fan Stippling is one of the easiest of the patterns to quilt, but the marking takes more time. Make a concentric compass by poking holes 1/4" apart along a line on a piece of cardboard or acetate. With a pin holding the end hole, mark the concentric arcs with a pencil. Once the arcs are all marked, quilt on the lines and once in between so the quilted lines are about 1/8" apart.

ECHO

To do echo or outline stippling, you do not need to mark, but you need to be careful what you are echoing. If the pattern is not intricate enough, your stippling will be boring and will also have a tendency to distort your quilt. When I do my stippled samplers, I choose the most intricate block to do the echo stippling. Outline the motif with quilting lines every 1/8" or closer. Avoid echo stippling in large unbroken areas.

Grape Vine Sampler, 17" x 22", John Flynn.

eveloping Designs

I look for quilting patterns everywhere. Architectural magazines are a great source especially with the renewed interest in metal ceilings. Most of these designs make ideal stippling and trapunto patterns. Fancy carved doors are another source for patterns. For my class work piece, pictured on page 30, I drew the grape-vine outside my window and superimposed a grid of window panes to create areas for six types of background stippling. The six blocks in "School Figures," pages 18-29, are all based on applique patterns from old quilts. For my sailing ships, I adapted drawings from encyclopedias and children's books.

Almost every building over fifty years old has some decorative wood or stone work that could be used for a quilting pattern. Headstones are an interesting source for quilting designs. Go to your public library and, if you get past the millwork on the entrance, pick books off the shelf at random and look for quilt designs. Look at covers, inside covers and at illuminated letters at the beginning of chapters. Somewhere in every book there's a quilting pattern. I never have had a problem developing a quilting pattern. In fact, I have more inspirations than time to use them.

Back to the Basics

While I do not intend this to be a "how to quilt" book,
a review of the "rules" is a good place to start. There are many
choices when planning and creating a quilt and every decision
will have an impact on the appearance of the quilt.

The Batting

Select your batting carefully. Spending an hour to choose your batting may seem like a lot at the time, but when you consider how many hours you will have to live with your decision, it seems more reasonable. I am notoriously remiss about documenting my batting choices, so this is a "do as I say, not as I do" instruction. Each time you make a quilt, write down in a safe place, a journal or a log, the batting used and how it was to quilt.

My experiences and preferences to the best of my recollection follow:

I do not choose a thick batt. I don't like a puffy look and I find it makes quilting more difficult. I use both cotton and poly batts depending on the individual project.

If I intend to wash the quilt when I am finished and if the quilting will be close together, I use a cotton batt because it is easier to get short stitches. A cotton batt requires more force to push the needle through the quilt. But, because the needle won't slip back out of the batt when there is a stitch on the tapered tip, I am able to make shorter stitches. Cotton fibers are shorter than poly fibers, so, while a cotton batt will beard, the fibers are much less noticeable. Cotton batts are more opaque than poly batts so the colors in the top remain true. Plus, we know how 100-year-old quilts with cotton batts have stood the test of time.

If I do not intend to wash the quilt after it is quilted, I use a light poly fiber batting because cotton batting stays matted down after quilting until it is washed. So if I don't intend to wash the piece, poly is my choice to provide enough relief to show off my quilting.

I avoid batts that are so dense that they are hard to needle and choose those that will beard the least or will show least when they do beard.

No matter what batt you choose, take a few minutes to prepare the batt properly before putting it into your quilt sandwich. Some batts have instructions on how to get all the wrinkles out. If not, your shop or quilt guild may have hints. If I have the patience, I spread the batt out the day before I put it into my quilt. Some poly batts can be fluffed in the dryer for a few minutes to get them to relax.

The Backing Fabric

The back can have as much effect on the final appearance of the quilt as the batting. If the backing fabric is much more loosely woven than the top, the majority of the relief will show on the back where the fabric stretches rather than on the front. If the back is too tightly woven or has a hard finish, it is difficult to get those tiny stitches. Unless I have good reason not to, I match the backing fabric and the fabrics in the top as closely as possible.

Tip: I suggest making a small 4" x 4" test square of your quilt sandwich. Try a little trapunto and stippling before you commit to the materials for a large project.

Marking

I mark my quilt top with the motifs and the background grids for stippling. If you haven't commited to your stippling pattern, you can mark the grids after you have finished the trapunto.

If I am working on an heirloom piece, I trace the motifs and rule the grid with a lead pencil. I use a mechanical pencil with a 0.3-mm thick, 4H lead. Because this is such a hard lead, the markings are very light and generally hidden by the stippling. If you use a softer lead, and it smears, remove it by lightly scrubbing the fabric with a soft toothbrush dipped in a solution of one part rubbing alcohol, two parts water and one or two drops of dishwashing liquid. Rinse the quilt thoroughly in water.

If I am working on an test piece, I transfer the motif and grids using a photocopy of the pattern. Lay the photocopy face down on the top and iron. The photocopy toner transfers to the quilt top. Because this requires added pressure, I iron on a padded tabletop rather than the ironing board for a more stable surface. (Be careful not to burn your tabletop.) Set the iron to a wool setting. Do not steam. The photocopy toner becomes tacky with the heat so there is no need to pin. All photocopies seem to work about the same, but it is a good idea to do a small test. REMEMBER, YOUR MOTIF IMAGE WILL BE REVERSED (A MIRROR IMAGE) SO PLAN ACCORDINGLY.

Basting

I know you don't want to, but you have to! Basting won't take long compared to how long your quilt is going to last. Careful basting can make the difference between a quilt that lays flat and hangs straight and one that doesn't.

I baste with an embroidery needle threaded with quilting thread a different color than I intend to use for quilting. I baste with a 3/4" plus stitch length on a 4" square grid. I work from the middle while the quilt sandwich hangs over the edges of my table. There are people who insist that the back be stretched as tight as a drum and then the batt and top laid on. As an engineer, this doesn't make sense to me. I think both top and back should be under the same tension to start. Some say the basting lines should be like the spokes of a wheel radiating from the middle of the quilt. This is fine, except it makes use of the Trapunto Rod difficult.

Choosing a Frame

There are nearly as many frame designs as there are quilt patterns. Opinions vary as to which design is best. No frame is ideal for every situation, so it is up to you to decide which frame best meets your needs.

I designed my lap scroll frame because I didn't have room for a floor frame at the time. After quilting on my frame for the past few years, I wouldn't trade it for a floor frame if I did have the room.

The trapunto technique discussed in this book will work with my frame or with any scroll-type floor frame, including the no-baste frames.

To fasten my quilt to the frame, I simply leave the back slightly longer than the top and staple the back to the rods with a desk stapler. Match the centers of the quilt to the centers of the rods.

The Quilting Stitch

*I am a self-taught hand quilter. My style is different
from any I have seen, but, the basic mechanics
of the quilt stitch are the same no matter
what style you use.*

Choose your needle. I use a Size 8 Between. This is considered large
by many quilters (most use a 10 or 12) but my hands are larger.
I can't get any better results with a tiny-eyed 12 than I do with my 8.
I use the one I am most comfortable with. You should, too.

Thread. I use Gutermann 100% cotton or Coats cotton covered polyester
because they tangle less. Some say quilting thread should be a weaker
all cotton thread so it will break before damaging the top if it is pulled.
I can't argue with this reasoning. I just prefer to quilt with a thread that
doesn't tangle.

Thread your needle with about eighteen inches of quilting thread.
Tie a single knot at the end you just cut from the spool.

Stitch Length. In many traditional quilt circles, there is a great preoccupation
with stitch length. The general consensus being that shorter stitches are better.
For my money, having an even stitch is most important. Stitch length is not
as important with the quality threads available today.

I remember my disappointment when I discovered that a quilting stitch
includes both the top and bottom stitch in the quilt. I was up to twelve
sitiches to the inch and going for the eighteen experts talk about when
I was informed I was only getting six stitches to the inch! Now, I get around
ten stitches to the inch and I really don't try to make them any shorter.

Stippling looks best when you get between 6 and 12 stitches to the inch.
If your stitches are longer or shorter, the patterns will not develop properly.
An even stitch is very important to the success of a stippling project.

Quilting

To start quilting, I tie a single knot in my thread and enter through the top about 3/4" from where I want my first stitch to be and travel inside the sandwich, through a seam if possible to hold the knot better. When the needle reaches the point I want to start quilting, I pull the needle through and "pop" the knot through the top so it is buried between the layers. Some quilters recommend starting through the back — try both ways and find what works best for you.

Step-by-step quilting using my method.

Theoretically, to keep your stitch even on the front and back, the needle should always pierce the quilt at a 90 degree angle — perpendicular to the quilt. It is easy to visualize the quilt as a flat surface and the needle moving through it. However, since the needle will not bend, the fabric will have to. I keep the needle fairly still and almost flat on the quilt and manipulate the quilt at the point of the needle — alternately pushing the quilt up and down in front of the advancing needle.

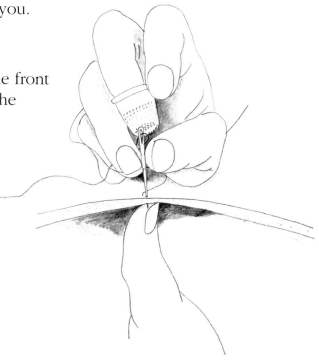

To start your first stitch, the needle should go through the quilt sandwich at a 90 degree angle.

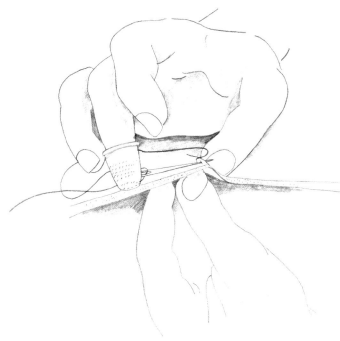

Drop the eye end of the needle to be parallel with the quilting line. Advance the needle point along the backing fabric half a stitch length and go through the sandwich at 90 degrees to the plane. Since the needle will not bend, I push the quilt top down 90 degrees at the point end of the needle.

You can stop now having completed one stitch and repeat the process but it has always been my opinion that the first stitch is the hard one and the next 5 or 6 are free

I continue by advancing the needle another half stitch length on top, then push the plane up 90 degrees from the bottom. Pierce the sandwich, advance half a stitch length on back, push the plane down 90 degrees from the top, pierce the sandwich...

Repeat until the needle is full or too hard to pull through.

Pull the needle
through
and repeat.

When you reach the end of your thread, finish off
by tying a knot at the surface of the quilt where
the last stitch ended. Re-enter the last hole and
weave the needle back along the quilting line
between the layers and pop the knot back
between the layers. Cut the thread off flush
and the end will slip back
between the layers.

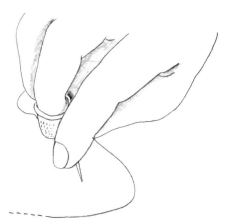

Note that the
quilting stitches
are set into the
surface of the quilt.
This tension is especially important
when stippling.

Trapunto will look great no matter what your quilting skill level.
Stippling will be much more effective if your stitches are even
and in the 6 - 12 to the inch range.

Patterns

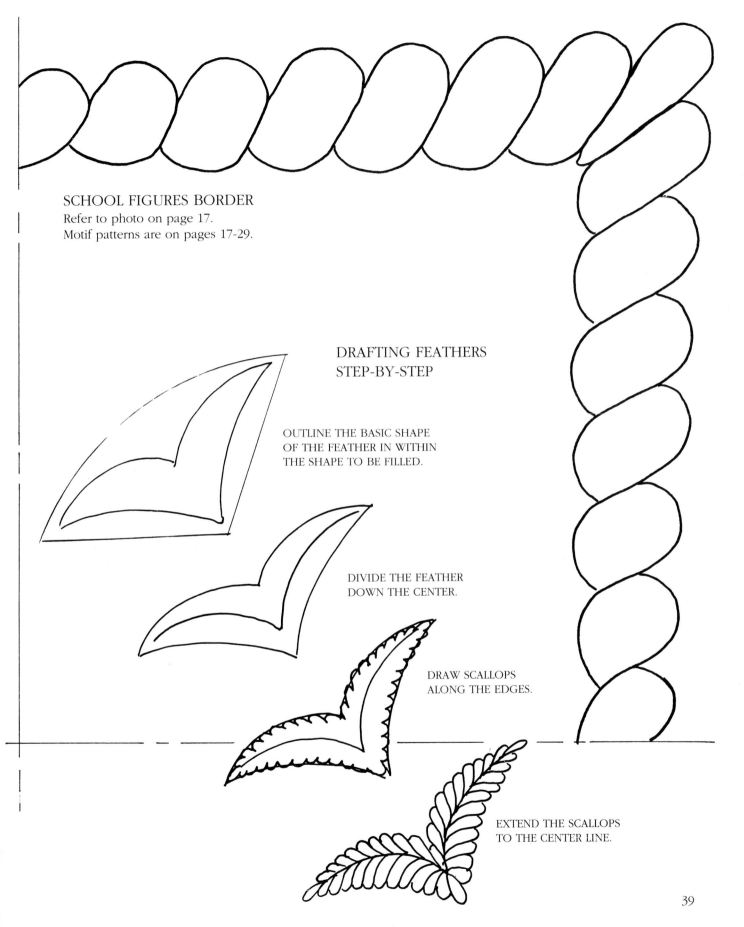

SCHOOL FIGURES BORDER
Refer to photo on page 17.
Motif patterns are on pages 17-29.

**DRAFTING FEATHERS
STEP-BY-STEP**

OUTLINE THE BASIC SHAPE
OF THE FEATHER IN WITHIN
THE SHAPE TO BE FILLED.

DIVIDE THE FEATHER
DOWN THE CENTER.

DRAW SCALLOPS
ALONG THE EDGES.

EXTEND THE SCALLOPS
TO THE CENTER LINE.

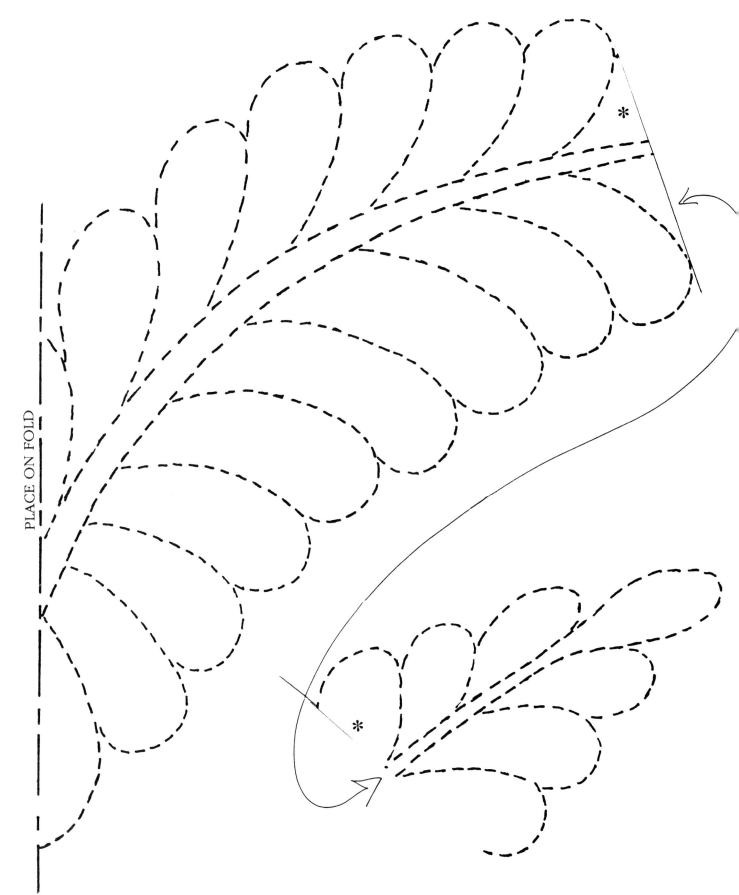

PLACE ON FOLD

*

*

GRAPE VINE SAMPLER

Enlarge border to fit. Actual size patterns for blocks begin on page 42.

SAILING SHIPS

BRIGANTINE

BRIG

TOPSAIL SCHOONER

SCHOONER

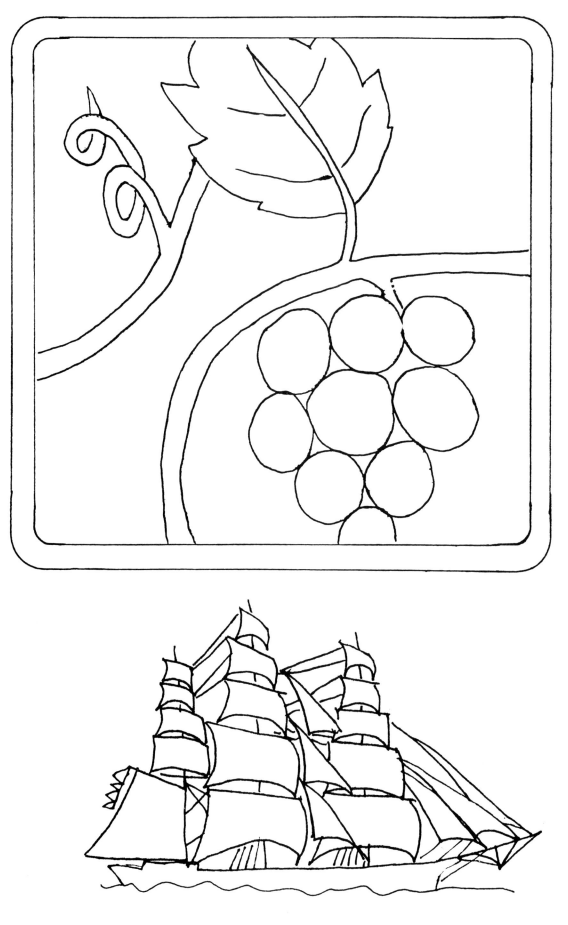

CLIPPER SHIP

BALTIMORE CLIPPER

*Look for Trapunto Rods
and Flynn Quilt Frames
at your local quilting shop.*

*Or, call or write for
more information and
a catalog.*

TOLL FREE 1-800-745-3596

1000 SHILOH OVERPASS ROAD
BILLINGS, MONTANA 59106

*Other Step-By-Step books
by John Flynn...*

Double Wedding Ring

Braided Borders

Texas Star Pattern